Real Mad Quiz Buun

101 Questions To Test Your Knowledge Of This Successful and Prestigious Football Club

Published by Glowworm Press
7 Nuffield Way
Abingdon, Oxfordshire OX14 1RL

By Chris Carpenter

Real Madrid

This book contains one hundred and one informative and entertaining trivia questions with multiple choice answers. With 101 questions, some easy, some more demanding, this entertaining book will really test your knowledge of Real Madrid Football Club.

You will be quizzed on a wide range of topics associated with Real Madrid CF for you to test yourself, with questions on players, managers, opponents, transfer deals, trophies, records, fixtures and more, guaranteeing you a truly educational experience. The **Real Madrid** Quiz Book will provide the ultimate in entertainment for fans of all ages and will certainly test your knowledge of this world famous club. The book is packed with information and is a must-have for Real Madrid supporters wherever you live.

2023/24 Season Edition

FOREWORD

When I was asked to write a foreword to this book I was flattered.

I have known the author Chris Carpenter for a number of years and his knowledge of facts and figures is phenomenal.

His love for football and his skill in writing quiz books make him the ideal man to pay homage to my great love Real Madrid CF.

This book came about as a result of a challenge on a golf course.

I do hope you enjoy the book.

Diego Garcia

Let's kick off with some relatively easy questions.

1. When was Real Madrid founded?
   A. 1900
   B. 1902
   C. 1904

2. What is Real Madrid's nickname?
   A. Los Baggies
   B. Los Banditos
   C. Los Blancos

3. Where does Real Madrid play their home games?
   A. Santiago Bernabeu
   B. Stadium of Light
   C. Vicente Calderon

4. What is the stadium's capacity?
   A. 81,186
   B. 82,186
   C. 83,186

5. Who has made the most appearances for the club in total?
   A. Iker Casillas
   B. Raul Gonzalez
   C. Manuel Sanchis

6. Who has made the most *League* appearances for the club?
   A. Iker Casillas
   B. Raul Gonzalez

C. Manuel Sanchis

7. Who is the club's record goal scorer?
   A. Raul Gonzalez
   B. Cristiano Ronaldo
   C. Hugo Sanchez

8. Who is the fastest ever goal scorer for the club?
   A. Emilio Butragueno
   B. Ronaldo
   C. Ivan Zamorano

9. What is the club's official website address?
   A. madrid.es
   B. realmadrid.com
   C. realmadridfc.es

10. Who or what is the club mascot?
   A. Indi the racoon
   B. Pingu the penguin
   C. No mascot

Here are the answers to the first ten questions. If you get eight or more right, you are doing very well so far, but the questions will get harder.

A1. Real Madrid was founded on 6th March 1902 as Madrid Football Club. The word *Real* is Spanish for *Royal* and was bestowed to the club by King Alfonso XIII in 1920.

A2. Real Madrid's nickname is Los Blancos. In English it means "The Whites".

A3. Real Madrid plays their home games at the Santiago Bernabeu Stadium.

A4. According to Wikipedia, the current stadium capacity is 82,186. After the current renovation is complete, it will hold close to 85,000 people.

A5. Raul has made the most appearances for the club in total. He played in 741 first-team matches from 1994 to 2010. Casillas holds the record for a goalkeeper with 725 appearances.

A6. Raul has made the most appearances for the club in La Liga, appearing 550 times. He is a true legend in Madrid.

A7. Cristiano Ronaldo is the all-time record goal scorer having scored 311 goals in his 292 appearances for the club! He was the fastest player to score 200 goals in La Liga, which he accomplished in his 178th La Liga game.

A8. Ivan Zamorano is the fastest ever goal scorer for the club. He scored just 12 seconds after kick off in a La Liga game against Sevilla on 3rd September 1994.

A9. realmadrid.com is the club's official website address.

A10. Although you may be able to track down cuddly toy bears wearing the club kit on eBay, there is no official club mascot.

OK, back to the questions.

11. What is the highest number of goals that Real Madrid has scored in a league season?
    A. 115
    B. 118
    C. 121

12. What is the fewest number of goals that Real Madrid has conceded in a league season?
    A. 13
    B. 15
    C. 17

13. What is the record number of points the club has ever achieved in a season?
    A. 96
    B. 98
    C. 100

14. What is the record number of goals scored in a season in all competitions?
    A. 134
    B. 154
    C. 174

15. Where did Real Madrid play their home games before the move to the Bernabeu?
    A. Estadio Chamartin
    B. Estadio Chantello
    C. Estadio Charablanco

16. When did Real Madrid move to the Santiago Bernabeu?
    A. 1927
    B. 1937
    C. 1947

17. What match was played at the stadium on 11th July 1982?
    A. Champions League Final
    B. Super Copa Final
    C. World Cup Final

18. What is the name of the road the ground is on?
    A. Avenida Concha Espina
    B. Calle Principe De Vergara
    C. Paseo de Juan XXIII

19. What is the size of the pitch?
    A. 105x62m
    B. 105x65m
    C. 105x68m

20. What is Real Madrid's training ground called?
    A. Ciudad Deportivo
    B. Ciudad Real Madrid
    C. Ciudad de Stefano

Here are the answers to the last set of questions.

A11. Real Madrid scored an incredible 121 goals in 38 matches in the 2011/12 season.

A12. Real Madrid conceded just 15 goals during the 1931/32 season.

A13. With Jose Mourinho as manager, the club amassed 100 points during the 2011/12 season.

A14. The club scored an amazing 174 goals in all competitions in the 2011/12 season.

A15. Real Madrid used to play at the Estadio Chamartin.

A16. Real Madrid played at Estadio Chamartin until 1947 when they moved into the Bernabeu. The Santiago Bernabeu Stadium as it is known today was inaugurated on 14th December 1947, although it did not acquire the present name until 1955.

A17. The Bernabeu played host to the 1982 World Cup Final on 11th July when Italy beat Germany 3-1. The stadium has also hosted four European Cup / Champions League finals, the most recent one in 2010 when Internazionale beat Bayern Munich 2-0.

A18. The ground is located on Avenida Concha Espina.

A19. The size of the pitch is 105 metres long by 68 metres wide, which is the UEFA recommended pitch size.

A20. Real Madrid's training ground is located outside Madrid in Valdebebas. It is known as Ciudad Real Madrid (Real Madrid City) and was inaugurated in September 2005.

Now we move onto some questions about the club's records.

21. What is the club's record win in any competition?
   A. 10-1
   B. 11-1
   C. 12-1

22. Who did they beat?
   A. Barcelona
   B. Deportivo La Coruna
   C. Real Betis

23. In which season?
   A. 1922/23
   B. 1932/33
   C. 1942/43

24. What is the club's record win in the league?
   A. 9-2
   B. 10-2
   C. 11-2

25. Who did they beat?
   A. Eibar
   B. Elche
   C. Espanyol

26. In which season?
   A. 1951/52
   B. 1955/56
   C. 1959/60

27. What is the club's record defeat?
    A. 0-8
    B. 1-8
    C. 0-9

28. Who has scored the most hat tricks in La Liga for Real Madrid?
    A. Raul Gonzalez
    B. Cristiano Ronaldo
    C. Hugo Sanchez

29. Who has scored the most hat tricks for Real Madrid in a single season?
    A. Francisco Gento
    B. Cristiano Ronaldo
    C. Carlos Santillana

30. How many people watched the match between Real Madrid and Manchester United in Chicago in 2014?
    A. 103,274
    B. 105,826
    C. 109,318

Here are the answers to the last set of questions.

A21. The club's record win in any competition is 11-1.

A22. The club beat Barcelona 11-1, and this is a source of great pride to Madrid fans.

A23. The match took place on 13th June 1943, during the 1942/43 Copa del Generalisimo.

A24. The club's record win in La Liga is 11-2.

A25. Real Madrid trashed Elche 11-2 to record their highest ever win in La Liga.

A26. The club beat Elche 11-2 on 7th February 1960, during the 1959/60 La Liga season.

A27. The club's record defeat in any competition is 1-8, when the club lost to Espanyol on 5th March 1930, during the 1929/30 La Liga season.

A28. Cristiano Ronaldo has scored the most hat tricks for the club – an incredible 34 hat tricks in La Liga in his time at the club. He has scored hat tricks against 19 different teams in La Liga!

A29. It's that man Cristiano Ronaldo again. He holds the record for the most number of hat tricks in a season. He scored eight hat tricks for the club in the 2014/15 season.

A30. On 2nd August 2014, 109,318 spectators watched a match between Real Madrid and Manchester United at Michigan Stadium in Chicago, which is a record crowd for a football match in the United States.

Now we move onto questions about the club's trophies.

31. How many times have Real Madrid won La Liga?
    A. 31
    B. 33
    C. 35

32. How many times have Real Madrid won the Copa del Rey?
    A. 14
    B. 17
    C. 20

33. How many times have Real Madrid won the Supercopa de Espana?
    A. 11
    B. 12
    C. 13

34. When did the club win their first La Liga title?
    A. 1911/12
    B. 1921/22
    C. 1931/32

35. When did the club win their first Copa Del Rey?
    A. 1905
    B. 1925
    C. 1935

36. When did the club win their first Supercopa de Espana?
    A. 1968

B. 1978
C. 1988

37. Who was the last captain to lift the La Liga trophy?
    A. Iker Casillas
    B. Marcelo
    C. Sergio Ramos

38. Who was the last captain who lifted the Copa del Rey?
    A. Karim Benzema
    B. Pepe
    C. Sergio Ramos

39. Who was the captain who lifted the 2020 Supercopa de Espana played in Saudi Arabia?
    A. Xabi Alonso
    B. Iker Casillas
    C. Sergio Ramos

40. How many Real Madrid players have won the Ballon d'Or award?
    A. 4
    B. 6
    C. 8

Here are the answers to the last block of questions.

A31. Real Madrid has won La Liga 35 times, most recently in the 2021/22 season.

A32. Real Madrid has won the Copa Del Rey (in English, the King's Cup) twenty times, most recently in 2023.

A33. The Supercopa de Espana is contested between the winners of La Liga and the Copa Del Rey of the previous season. It is normally played in August. Real Madrid has won the Supercopa de Espana twelve times, most recently in 2022.

A34. Real Madrid won their first La Liga title at the end of the 1931/32 season.

A35. Real Madrid won their first Copa Del Rey in 1905.

A36. Real Madrid won their first Supercopa de Espana in 1988, six years after the competition's formation.

A37. Marcelo was the club captain who last lifted La Liga trophy at the end of the 2021/22 season.

A38. Karim Benzema was the captain who lifted the Copa Del Rey on 6th May 2023 after a 2-1 victory over Osasuna at the La Cartuja Stadium in Seville.

A39. Sergio Ramos lifted the 2020 Supercopa in Jeddah, Saudi Arabia on 12th January 2020, after Real Madrid had beaten Atlético 4-1 on penalties after a 0-0 draw.

A40. The following players have won the Ballon d'Or (Golden Ball) award while playing for Real Madrid: Alfredo Di Stefano in 1957 and 1959; Raymond Kopa in 1958; Luis Figo in 2000; Ronaldo in 2002; Fabio Cannavaro in 2006; Cristiano Ronaldo in 2013, 2014, 2016 and 2017, Luka Modric in 2018 and Karim Benzema in 2022. That is a total of eight players.

I hope you're having fun and getting most of the answers right.

41. What is the record transfer fee paid?
    A. €83 million
    B. €93 million
    C. €103 million

42. Who was the record transfer fee paid for?
    A. Gareth Bale
    B. Jude Bellingham
    C. Eden Hazard

43. What is the record transfer fee received?
    A. €80 million
    B. €90 million
    C. €100 million

44. Who was the record transfer fee received for?
    A. Angel di Maria
    B. Alvaro Morata
    C. Cristiano Ronaldo

45. Who has won the most international caps whilst a Real Madrid player?
    A. Iker Casillas
    B. Raul
    C. Zinedine Zidane

46. Who scored the most international goals whilst a Real Madrid player?
    A. Raul

B. Cristiano Ronaldo

C. Alfredo di Stefano

47. Who is the youngest player ever to represent the club?

A. Marc Odergard

B. Mario Odergard

C. Martin Odergard

48. Who is Real Madrid's youngest ever goal scorer?

A. Carlos Alberto

B. Roberto Carlos

C. Alberto Rivera

49. Who is the oldest player ever to represent the club?

A. Fernando Morientes

B. Ferenc Puskas

C. Zinedine Zidane

50. Who is Real Madrid's oldest post-war goal scorer?

A. Ferenc Puskas

B. Hugo Sanchez

C. Carlos Santillana

Here are the answers to the last set of questions.

A41. Real Madrid's record transfer fee paid is €103 million.

A42. Real Madrid paid €103 million for Englishman Jude Bellingham, who moved from Borussia Dortmund in June 2023.

A43. The record transfer fee received by Real Madrid is €100 million.

A44. The record fee was received for Cristiano Ronaldo when he was sold to Juventus on 10th July 2018.

A45. Iker Casillas won 162 caps for Spain while he was at Real Madrid, which is the highest for a player whilst at the club.

A46. Ronaldo has scored the most international goals whilst a Real Madrid player; with 63 in total. Raul Gonzalez is in second place, having scored 44 international goals whilst a Real Madrid player.

A47. Martin Odergard is the youngest player ever to represent the club. He made his first team appearance at the age of 16 years, 157 days against Getafe on 23rd May 2015.

A48. Alberto Rivera became the club's youngest ever goalscorer when he scored against Celta Vigo in La Liga on 10th June 1995 aged just 17 years and 114 days.

A49. Ferenc Puskas is the oldest player ever to represent the club appearing against Sevilla on 21st November 1965 in La Liga aged an incredible 38 years and 233 days. He joined the club aged 31 from Honved Budapest.

A50. Ferenc Puskas is also Real Madrid's oldest goal scorer, scoring against Sevilla on 21st November 1965 aged 38 years and 233 days. Puskas was a prolific goal scorer; he represented Hungary 85 times and scored 84 goals.

I hope you're learning some new facts about the club, and here is the next set of questions.

51. Who was the first Real Madrid player to play for Spain?
    A. Juan Mondrian
    B. Juan Monjardin
    C. Juan Monmartre

52. Who was the first manager of the club?
    A. Juan de Carcer
    B. Arthur Johnson
    C. Pedro Llorente

53. Who is the club's longest serving manager of all time?
    A. Leo Beenhakker
    B. Vicente del Bosque
    C. Miguel Munoz

54. Which of these men won the Champions League whilst manager at the club?
    A. Rafael Benitez
    B. Vicente del Bosque
    C. Bernd Schuster

55. Fabio Capello has managed the club on two separate occasions. What is his nationality?
    A. Italian
    B. Portuguese
    C. Spanish

56. Which ex-manager went on to manage Spain?
- A. Vicente del Bosque
- B. Benito Floro
- C. Juande Ramos

57. What is on top of the club crest?
- A. Crown
- B. Flag
- C. Lion

58. What colour is the stripe on the club badge?
- A. Blueberry
- B. Mulberry
- C. Raspberry

59. What is the club's motto?
- A. Consectatio Excellentiae
- B. Labor omnia vincit
- C. No motto

60. Who is considered as Real Madrid's main rivals?
- A. Barcelona
- B. Celta Vigo
- C. Valencia

Here are the answers to the last set of questions.

A51. Juan Monjardin was the first Real Madrid player to play for Spain, making his debut against Portugal on 17th December 1922.

A52. Englishman Arthur Johnson was Real Madrid's first manager, serving the club from 1910 to 1920.

A53. Miguel Munoz is the club's longest serving manager of all time. He served for 15 years in two spells from February to April 1959 and from April 1960 to January 1974. He managed 595 games in total. It is a record that is unlikely to be broken.

A54. The club won the Champions League twice with Vicente Del Bosque as manager, in 2000 and 2002.

A55. Capello was born near Venice, in Italy. In his first spell at the club he managed for 48 games; and in his second spell 50 games.

A56. Vicente Del Bosque went on to manage Spain and he delivered the country its first ever World Cup, in 2010.

A57. A crown sits on top of the crest.

A58. The mulberry stripe of Castile has historically been used on the club crest, but this has recently been adapted to be more blue in colour.

A59. Oddly, Real Madrid does not have an official motto.

A60. Some people in Madrid feel that Atletico is their main rival, but the general consensus is that Barcelona are considered to be Real Madrid's main rival. Real Madrid contests the "El Clasico" derby with them. It is arguably the biggest club match in world football.

Let's give you some easier questions.

61. What is the traditional colour of the home shirt?
   - A. Cream
   - B. Red and white stripes
   - C. White

62. What is the traditional colour of the away shirt?
   - A. Black
   - B. Blue
   - C. Green

63. Who is the current club shirt sponsor?
   - A. Emirates
   - B. Etihad
   - C. Qatar Airways

64. Who was the first club shirt sponsor?
   - A. bwin
   - B. Parmalat
   - C. Zanussi

65. Which of these once sponsored the club?
   - A. Samsung
   - B. Siemens
   - C. Sony

66. Who currently supplies kit to the club?
   - A. Adidas
   - B. Hummel
   - C. Nike

67. Which of these has never supplied kit to the club?
  A. Hummel
  B. Kelme
  C. Nike

68. Who is currently the club president?
  A. Vicente Boluda
  B. Ramon Calderon
  C. Florentino Perez

69. Who was the previous club president?
  A. Vicente Boluda
  B. Ramon Calderon
  C. Florentino Perez

70. What is the club's official twitter account?
  A. @RealMadrid
  B. @RealMadridCF
  C. @RMCF

Here are the answers to the last ten questions.

A61. The traditional colour of the home shirt is of course white.

A62. Since the advent of the replica kit market, the club has released all manner of one colour designs including red, green, orange and black. However, Real's traditional away colours are historically all blue or all purple.

A63. Emirates is the current shirt sponsor of Real Madrid.

A64. Italian white goods manufacturer Zanussi was the first shirt sponsor of Real Madrid, back in 1982.

A65. Siemens sponsored the club in various guises from 2002 until 2007, first as Siemens, then Siemens mobile and finally as BenQ-Siemens.

A66. Adidas is the current kit supplier to the club and has been since 1998.

A67. Nike has never supplied kit to the club, whereas Hummel and Kelme have.

A68. Florentino Perez has been the club president since 1st June 2009. This is his second spell as president, having previously been in office from 2000 to 2006. Incidentally, his personal net worth is estimated at over 2 billion Euros.

A69. Perez took over from Vicente Boluda, who was president for a short period, from January to May 2009.

A70. @RealMadrid is the club's official twitter account. It tweets multiple times daily and it now has almost 50 million followers worldwide.

Here are some questions about the club's achievements in European football.

71. How many times have Real Madrid won the European Cup / Champions League?
    A. 12
    B. 13
    C. 14

72. Who was the club's first European Cup final victory against?
    A. Benfica
    B. AC Milan
    C. Reims

73. Who was the club's last Champions League final victory against?
    A. Atletico
    B. Juventus
    C. Liverpool

74. Who did they beat 7-3 in the 1960 European Cup Final?
    A. Barcelona
    B. Eintracht Frankfurt
    C. Glasgow Celtic

75. Who scored a hat trick in the 1960 European Cup Final?
    A. Ferenc Puskas
    B. Alfredo di Stefano
    C. Both

76. Who was the manager of the side that won the European Cup in 1960?
   A. Miguel Munoz
   B. Jose Santamaria
   C. Jose Villalonga

77. Who was the manager of the side that won the Champions League (the decima) in 2014?
   A. Carlo Ancelotti
   B. Rafael Benitez
   C. Manuel Pellegrini

78. Who was the manager of the side that won the Champions League in 2018?
   A. Carlo Ancelotti
   B. Rafael Benitez
   C. Zinedine Zidane

79. How many of the five penalty takers scored in the 2016 Champions League Final penalty shoot-out?
   A. Three
   B. Four
   C. Five

80. Which club has Real Madrid played more matches against than any other in European competition?
   A. Bayern Munich
   B. Juventus
   C. AC Milan

Here are the answers to the last set of questions.

A71. Real Madrid has won the European Cup/Champions League trophy a record fourteen times. This is far more than any other club.

A72. In the first European Cup ever held, Real Madrid defeated FC Reims of France 4-3 in the final in Paris on 13th June 1956.

A73. Real Madrid beat Liverpool 1-0 in the 2022 Champions League Final on 28th May at the Stade de France in Paris.

A74. In what many people believe to be the greatest football match ever, on May 18th, 1960, Real Madrid beat Frankfurt 7-3 in front of 127,621 spectators at Hampden Park in Glasgow.

A75. Both Puskas and di Stefano scored hat tricks in the game.

A76. Miguel Munoz was the manager of the 1960 European Cup winning side. It was the fifth season in a row that the club had won the European Cup. After these five consecutive successes, Real was permanently awarded the original cup, and earnt the right to wear the UEFA 'badge of honour' on their shirts.

A77. Carlo Ancelotti was the manager of the 2014 Champions League winning side. He was the manager who delivered "the decima"; "the tenth" European

Cup/Champions League trophy that had proved so elusive to the club for so long. At the Stadio da Luz in Lisbon on 24th May 2014, the final score was Real Madrid 4 Atletico Madrid 1. But that doesn't tell the whole story. After 93 minutes, Real Madrid was trailing 0-1, until the last attack of the game.

A78. Zinedine Zidane was the manager of the 2018 Champions League winning side. He was appointed manager on 4th January 2016, and he led the club to a record three successive Champions League trophies.

A79. After the 2016 Champions League final between Atletico and Real Madrid finished 1-1 after normal time and extra time, it went to a penalty shoot-out. All five of the Real Madrid penalty takers scored enabling the club to win the shoot-out 5-3.

A80. Bayern Munch has been Real Madrid's opponents in European competition more than any other club. Real Madrid versus Bayern Munich is also the match that has been played most often in the Champions League era. Madrid supporters often refer to Bayern as the "Bestia Negra" ("Black Beast").

Here are the next set of questions, let's hope you get most of them right.

81. Who was the first player to score five goals in a league match for the club?
    A. Manuel Alday
    B. Antonio Alsua
    C. Jorge Benguria

82. Who was nicknamed "The Blonde Arrow"?
    A. David Beckham
    B. Ferenc Puskas
    C. Alfredo di Stefano

83. Which forward was nicknamed "Pancho"?
    A. Kaka
    B. Ferenc Puskas
    C. Robinho

84. How many times have the club won the FIFA Club World Cup?
    A. 4
    B. 6
    C. 8

85. What nationality is Toni Kroos?
    A. Dutch
    B. German
    C. Swiss

86. What transfer fee was received from Chelsea for defensive midfielder Claude Makelele?

A. £12.8 million
B. £14.8 million
C. £16.8 million

87. What shirt number does Luka Modric wear?
A. 10
B. 14
C. 19

88. How many times have the club won the European Super Cup?
A. 3
B. 5
C. 7

89. What nationality is Luis Figo?
A. French
B. Italian
C. Portuguese

90. What shirt number did Zinedine Zidane wear?
A. 4
B. 5
C. 6

Here are the answers to the last set of questions.

A81. Manuel Alday was the first player to score five goals in a league match for the club. He scored five goals against Espanyol in a La Liga match on the 28th February 1943.

A82. Alfredo di Stefano was nicknamed "La Saeta Rubia" or in English "The Blonde Arrow".

A83. Puskas was nicknamed "Pancho" and also 'Canoncito pum".

A84. The club has won the FIFA Club World Club Cup a record eight times.

A85. Toni Kroos was born in Greifswald in Germany.

A86. £16.8 million was received for Makelele from Chelsea in the summer of 2003. Zidane said at the time that Madrid had lost the engine room of the team. Then Chelsea manager Claudio Ranieri stated that Makelele would become the "battery" of the team.

A87. Modric now wears shirt number 10 for Real Madrid. He used to wear number 19.

A88. The club has won the European Super Cup a record five times.

A89. Luis Figo was born in Almada, Portugal.

A90. Zidane wore shirt number 5 for Real Madrid.

Here is the final set of questions. Enjoy!

91. What was the name given to the expensive elite footballers acquired in the early 2000s?
    A. Galacticos
    B. Exclusivos
    C. Magnificos

92. In December 2014, the club extended their winning streak to how many games?
    A. 20
    B. 24
    C. 28

93. In the 1980s who was nicknamed "El Buitre" (The Vulture)?
    A. Emilio Butragueno
    B. Michel
    C. Rafael Martin Vazquez

94. Who made a record 171 consecutive League appearances for the club?
    A. Ike Casillas
    B. Guti
    C. Alfredo di Stefano

95. Who made the most appearances in European competitions whilst a Real Madrid player?
    A. Iker Casillas
    B. Raul
    C. Zinedine Zidane

96. Cristiano Ronaldo holds the record for most goals in a single Champions League season. How many goals did he score?
   A. 13
   B. 15
   C. 17

97. To which club was Mesut Ozil sold to in September 2013?
   A. Arsenal
   B. Paris Saint Germain
   C. Werder Bremen

98. How many players have won the European Golden Shoe award whilst at the club?
   A. 2
   B. 3
   C. 4

99. What position does the club hold in the latest IFFHS Club World Ranking?
   A. 1st
   B. 2nd
   C. 3rd

100. What is the Real Madrid Academy known as?
   A. La Fabrica
   B. La Factoria
   C. La Fantasia

101. Which of the following is the club anthem?
- A. De las glorias deportivas
- B. Hola Madrid
- C. Himno del Real Madrid

Here are the answers to the final set of questions.

A91. Between 2000 and 2006 the club paid extremely high transfer fees for elite footballers such as Beckham, Cannavaro, Figo, Ronaldo and Zidane and the team became known as Los Galacticos.

A92. In December 2014, the club extended their winning streak to 22 games with a 2-0 win over San Lorenzo in the 2014 FIFA World Club World Cup Final, thus ending the calendar year with four trophies.

A93. Butragueno was nicknamed El Buitre - the vulture. He was the leader of the so called La Quinta Del Buitre "The Vulture's Cohort".

A94. Alfredo di Stefano made 171 consecutive league appearances form 27th September 1953 to 22nd February 1959 - an incredible 5 years and 148 days.

A95. It's that man Casillas again, who made an incredible 155 appearances in European competition for the club.

A96. In the 2013/14 season, Cristiano scored a record breaking 17 goals in the Champions League campaign. That was 17 goals in 11 Champions League games in one season. Legend.

A97. Real Madrid bought Ozil from Werder Bremen for £12.3 million in August 2010 and sold him to Arsenal for £42.5 million in September 2013.

A98. The European Golden Shoe, formerly European Golden Boot, is awarded to the leading goal scorer in league matches in the top division of every European national league. Surprisingly just two players have won the European Golden Shoe while playing for Real Madrid: Hugo Sanchez in 1990 and Cristiano Ronaldo in 2011, 2014 and 2015.

A99. Since 1991 The International Federation of Football History and Statistics has produced a league table of club ranking, and this year, Real Madrid once again topped the list.

A100. Real Madrid's youth academy is known as La Fabrica.

A101. The club anthem is "Himno Del Real Madrid". The chorus is "Hala Madrid" which translates as "Forward Madrid" or "Come on Madrid".

That's it. That's a great question to finish with. I hope you enjoyed this book, and I hope you got most of the answers right.

I also hope you learnt some new facts about the club, and if you spotted anything wrong, or have a general comment, please visit the glowwormpress.com website and send us a message.

Thanks for reading, and if you did enjoy the book, would you please leave a positive review on Amazon.

Printed in Great Britain
by Amazon

43841890R00030